A Latter-Day Saint Guide to The ORIGINAL CHURCH of Jesus Christ

Find out what the original church taught, believed and practiced by a search of the Holy Bible

Copyright Media Literacy Consulting
All rights Reserved

No part of this book may be reproduced in any form by photocopying or any electronic or mechanical means including information storage or retreival systems, without permission in writing from the copyright owner and publisher of the book.

medialiteracyconsultancy@gmail.com

One Lord, One Faith, One Baptism

If there was originally one true Church of Jesus Christ when Jesus left his Apostles, how come so many 'Christian' denominations exist today, and why don't they all agree with eachother? Surely they all believe in the same Jesus Christ - don't they?

When Jesus was on the earth, and formed his true, one Church - there was no arguments amongst the believers. They were able to listen to Jesus as he preached, and they wrote down the doctrine - all the beliefs of the early Church.

When Jesus ascended into Heaven, and left his twelve apostles on the earth to run the new Church of Jesus Christ - he didn't leave them alone. He sent the Gift of the Holy Ghost to be a constant companion, a comfort, and a guide.

In those early days, without Jesus, the apostles met together often to organise the Church, to administer those things they had been taught, and to discuss the beliefs of Christ's Church.

But, as they spread across the land, building up the Church as they went, they were not able to meet together as often. And, because there were only 12 of them - trying to set up the Church in many areas - and different countries - they also were not able to meet with all the members of the new Church.

Communication wasn't like it is today, and messages took a long time to get to the different Church leaders. Sometimes, when there was a question about a particular belief, there would be a disagreement. Some members would think that Jesus had taught about that matter in one way, while others thought it had been taught a different way. You can see why there might have been splits in the Church that Jesus had set up.

As you know, in that early Church there was a lot of opposition. People thought that when Jesus was crucified, the Church would end with his death. They were annoyed to see it continue, and began to attack the apostles, and early Church leaders.

Soon, with the apostles spread across the world, unable to meet together, and with constant attacks on the leaders and even members of the Church, there soon arose a lot of disagreement.

People, who wanted to follow the teachings of Jesus, but saw the disagreements within the different congregations, found it hard to try to know and follow what was true. Even leaders became confused about what Jesus may or may not have taught.

There were some writings of what Jesus had taught while on the earth, but they weren't complete. They didn't even have the Bible that we have today - so they had to rely on eachother, and memories, to keep the early Church together. It wasn't easy, and soon, different branches of that original church started to go off alone, and set up their own groups. While the different church groups all believed in Jesus, and their members were faithful and wanted to follow Jesus, their leaders didn't all agree on the same beliefs.

With no apostles alive anymore, and new ones had not been able to be called to replace them, the different leaders continued to do their best to follow the techings of Jesus - but without direction from living apostles - who had received their instruction from Jesus Christ himself - there was no longer direct revelation from God.

And so, from that original one Lord, One faith Church that Jesus organised on the earth - there slowly developed dozens of different Christian religions, then hundreds, and now, today, we have over **45,000 different denominations - all claiming to be Christian** - but having different beliefs! That's crazy! Jesus didn't set up 45,000 different faiths - he said there should be just one.

So, which one - if any - is true? How can you tell? They all can't be teaching the truth, if they all differ about even the basics, like how should you be baptised, and by who? What is the Gift of the Holy Ghost? How do you become a priest or other church leader? Who has the authority of God, and who speaks for God today? It can be so confusing to know - which of all the churches out there - which one - if any - is the true and only Church of Jesus Christ.

Can God - our loving Heavenly Father- help us find the truth? Yes, he has given us dozens of clues - in our very own scriptures - the Holy Bible.

The Bible has the answers. It is a collection of writing from the old and new testament. But, more important are the very words and deeds of Jesus while he was on the earth. He set up a church - the original church - and if we want to know what that original church looked like - we only have to read the scriptures to find what exactly Jesus taught in the Original Church.

Is there any church today that looks like that original church, and teaches ALL the principles and beliefs taught by Jesus when he was on the earth?

To find a church that looks like, feels like, and is that exact same original church, any good Christian would want to find the answers by looking in their Holy Bible.

We will use the commonly found King James version of the Holy Bible because it is used by many Christian religions today. We will look together at that early Church, how it was set up, organized, and what Jesus and his early apostles taught.

The Bible doesn't contain all the writing of Jesus and his apostles - but it does contain enough for us to be able to pick out the most importance teachings of the early church - and ask ourselves - does this church still exist today?

As A Christian, and a seeker of truth, you will want to search diligently the writings of those who were in the original church - who taught the principles - and lived the way Jesus taught them to live.

We hope this book will help you in your search to find the original church of Jesus Christ, so that you can live the principles taught by the Saviour.

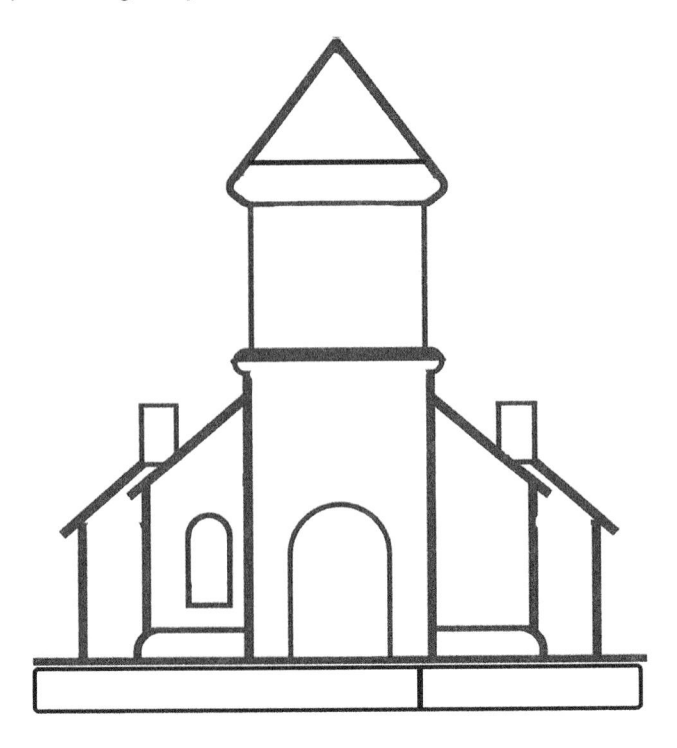

The Organization of the Original Church

When the Church was originally organized, members of the church were called to different positions within the church. In **Ephesians 4:11-14** we read:

11 And he gave some, apostles; and some, prophets; and some, evangelists; and some, pastors and teachers;

12 For the perfecting of the saints, for the work of the ministry, for the edifying of the body of Christ:

13 Till we all come in the unity of the faith, and of the knowledge of the Son of God, unto a perfect man, unto the measure of the stature of the fulness of Christ:

14 That we henceforth be no more children, tossed to and fro, and carried about with every wind of doctrine, by the sleight of men, and cunning craftiness, whereby they lie in wait to deceive;

Let's be clear about the positions within that early church. There were:

Apostles
Prophets
Evangelists
Pastors
Teachers

Verse 12 tells us that they were to work together to unify the church and edify Jesus, and verse 13 tells us that they were to help the church come together in unity of the faith. One faith.

Verse 14 is very important. The reason there were to be

Prophets and Apostles in the Church, was so that the members would not be led astray by men, by their cunning and craftiness. It warns that, without the leadershiip of Apostles and Prophets, men would "lie in wait to deceive." It means that without Prophets and Apostles in the church, men would lead the members astray - and would not have the powerful direct guidance from God.

Apostles and Prophets

That's exactly what happened. When the Apostles and Prophets were killed off, or died in that original church - they were not replaced - and the church was no longer led by them - as it was always meant to.

The Holy Bible tells us clearly here that without Prophets and Apostles at the head of the church - to lead by direct inspiration, or revelation from God - that men would lead the church away from the truths of God.

Are there any other places in the New Testament that talk about that original church foundation? Yes.in **Ephesians 5:23** Paul says:

19 Now therefore ye are no more strangers and foreigners, but fellowcitizens with the saints, and of the household of God;

20 And are built upon the foundation of the apostles and prophets, Jesus Christ himself being the chief corner stone;

Talking about the early members of the church this scripture says that when we join we are no more strangers, but that we are joined together in one, and that we (the church) are built upon a **foundation of Prophets and Apostles.**

So, again, the new testament tells us that the original church was built upon a foundation of Prophets and Apostles. Without a foundation, a building collapses, and that's exactly what happened to the original church after the first Apostles and Prophets were either killed, or died, and were not replaced.

Some people have argued that the original foundation of the early church was not supposed to last, that Jesus only selected 12 original apostles - and that after they died - they were not to be replaced. That is simply not true. This foundation of the Church was meant to continue forever.

Do you remember the first of the Apostles to leave the 12? It was Judas Iscariot, who betrayed Jesus. Was he replaced after he left? If there were only ever meant to be the original 12, then it would have ended there with no replacement for Judas.

However, there were always meant to be twelve apostles. The Church could not carry on without that firm foundation. And so, we read in the New Testament about the other Apostles gathering to replace Judas.

In Acts 1:23-26

23 And they appointed two, Joseph called Barsabas, who was surnamed Justus, and Matthias.

24 And they prayed, and said, Thou, Lord, which knowest the hearts of all men, shew whether of these two thou hast chosen,

25 That he may take part of this ministry and apostleship, from which Judas by transgression fell, that he might go to his own place.

26 And they gave forth their lots; and the lot fell upon Matthias; and he was numbered with the eleven apostles.

The eleven Apostles gathered together to replace Judas. They prayed to God to guide them as they cast lots, and it fell upon Matthias to be numbered with the eleven. There was always meant to be twelve apostles, because the church was built upon that foundation - with Jesus Christ being the chief cornerstone.

In the Old Testament, **Amos 3:7** tells us that *"Surely, the Lord God will do NOTHING except he revealeth His secrets unto his servants the Prophets."*

God will do NOTHING unless he does it through His Prophets. We need a Church today that has Prophets who receive direct revelation from God. If there are no Prophets how can the Church know the will of God?

The Original Church had Apostles and Prophets.

Does a church exist today that is built upon a foundation of **Apostles and Prophets** - with Jesus Christ as the chief cornerstone?

Apostles and Prophets	Jesus Christ

This was the very foundation upon which the Original Church of Jesus Christ was built.

In **Ephesians 5:23** we read about whose church it is.

23 For the husband is the head of the wife, even as Christ is the head of the church: and he is the saviour of the body.

Although Prophets and Apostles lead the Church on earth, the scriptures clearly say that Christ is the head of the Church, and the Chief Cornerstone.

It was His church - in His name. It was **The Church of Jesus Christ** - and was not called by any other name. It was not Paul's Church, it was not Mary's Church or Peter's Church. It wasn't Baptist, Pentecostal, Catholic, Protestant, Methodist - or any other name. It was then, and should be now, **The Church of Jesus Christ**.

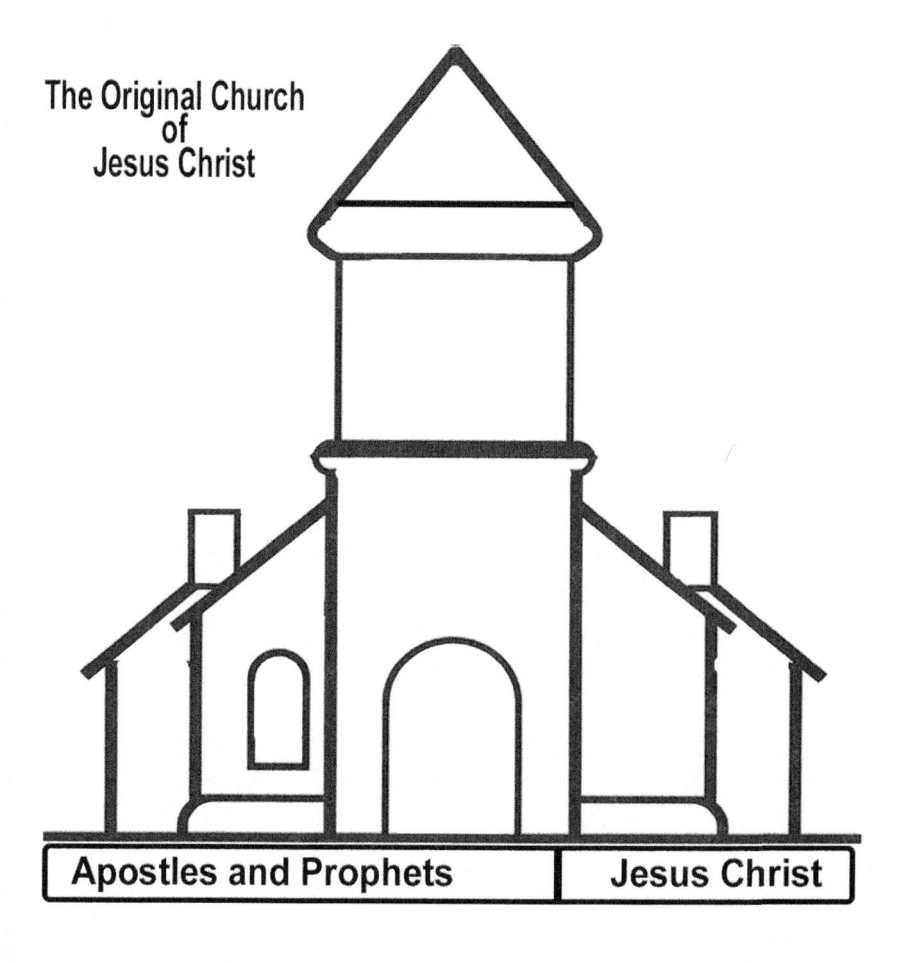

The Original Church
of
Jesus Christ

| Apostles and Prophets | Jesus Christ |

The Church Leaders Had Divine Authority - from God

To act in God's name, the early Apostles had to hold the correct authority, or The Priesthood of God. Everything they performed, they did so in the name of Jesus Christ, using the pristhood of God, which was given to them by Jesus. As the Apostles spread out to create other branches of the chruch in different areas, they would appoint local leaders and give them this authority which they held. They would pass it on.

No Leader could call themselves, they had to be called by one who already held that authority, and it was given to them by someone who held that authority.

This is really important. You cannot just wake up and say that God has called you to the work, or feel that you are called to be a preacher or priest. You MUST be called by someone who holds that authority, that has had it passed down to them from someone who held that authority - or priesthood.

In **Hebrews 5:4-10** we read about two different priesthoods. These are the only two kinds of priesthood that were held in the original church. One was the priesthood of Aaron (Aaronic priesthood) and the other was the Melchisedec Priesthood. There is no other priesthood. The original church leaders were given either the Aaronic Priesthood, or the Melchisedec Priesthood.

4 And no man taketh this honour unto himself, but he that is called of God, as was Aaron.

5 So also Christ glorified not himself to be made an high priest; but he that said unto him, Thou art my Son, to day have I begotten thee.

6 As he saith also in another place, Thou art a priest for ever after the order of Melchisedec.

7 Who in the days of his flesh, when he had offered up prayers and supplications with strong crying and tears unto him that was able to save him from death, and was heard in that he feared;

8 Though he were a Son, yet learned he obedience by the things which he suffered;

9 And being made perfect, he became the author of eternal salvation unto all them that obey him;

10 Called of God an high priest after the order of Melchisedec.

This scripture can be a bit difficult to follow, but it starts by saying that no man can take on the honour by himself. You cannot be self appointed, or self called. And, you must either be called, like Aaron (Aaronic Priesthood), or be called like Jesus himself - to the higher priesthood of Melchisedec.

Yes, Jesus himself held the Melchedidec priesthood. All the miracles he perfomed were done using the Melchisedec Pristhood.

Anyone who acted on behalf of Jesus in His church had to hold either one of these two priethood authorities. There was and is no other priesthood authority. If a leader wanted to call someone to a position he had to hold that priesthood authority.

If he wanted to baptize someone, or bestow the Gift of the Holy Ghost, he had to hold the correct priesthood authority - after being called by God - and having it passed down to him by someone who held that priesthood authority. This is the way that Jesus taught in His original church.

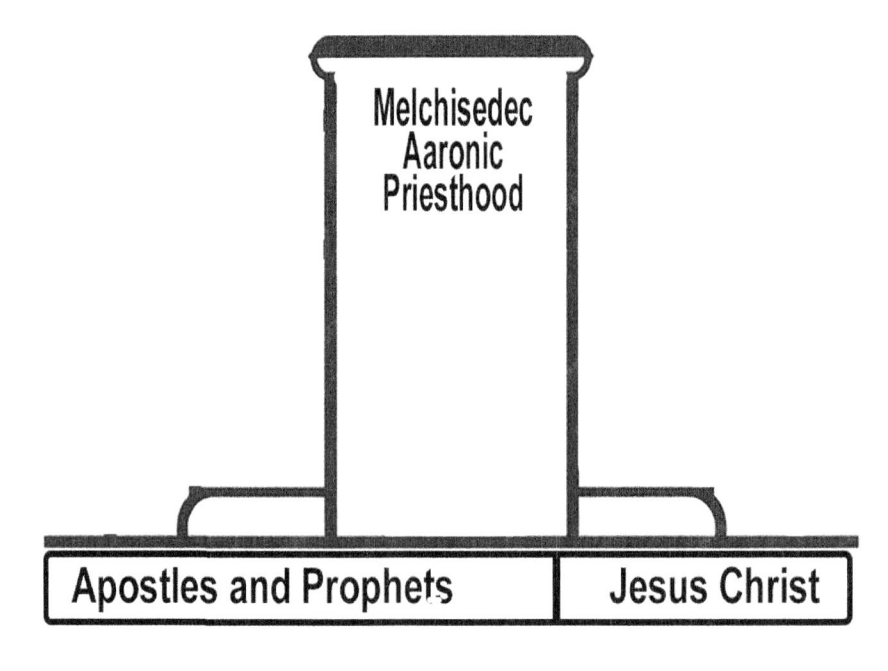

```
        ┌─────────────────┐
        │  Melchisedec    │
        │    Aaronic      │
        │   Priesthood    │
        │                 │
        │                 │
┌───────┴─────────────────┴───────┐
│ Apostles and Prophets │ Jesus Christ │
└───────────────────────┴──────────────┘
```

When the early Apostles were no longer able to meet together and pass the priesthood on, and as leaders spread out and were killed, or died, they were no longer able to keep passing on the correct priesthood authority in the correct way. Soon, the Aaronic and Melchisedec Priesthood were both lost from the earth. Therefore, the authority to act in the name of God and Jesus was lost.

Without the Priesthood, no new Elders could be called, no Baptsims could be carried out with the right authority, no one could bestow the Gift of the Holy Ghost without the correct Priesthood handed down, and no other acttion could be done within the Church - because the correct Pristhood authority no longer existed.

Melchisedec
Aaronic
Priesthood

Laying on of Hands

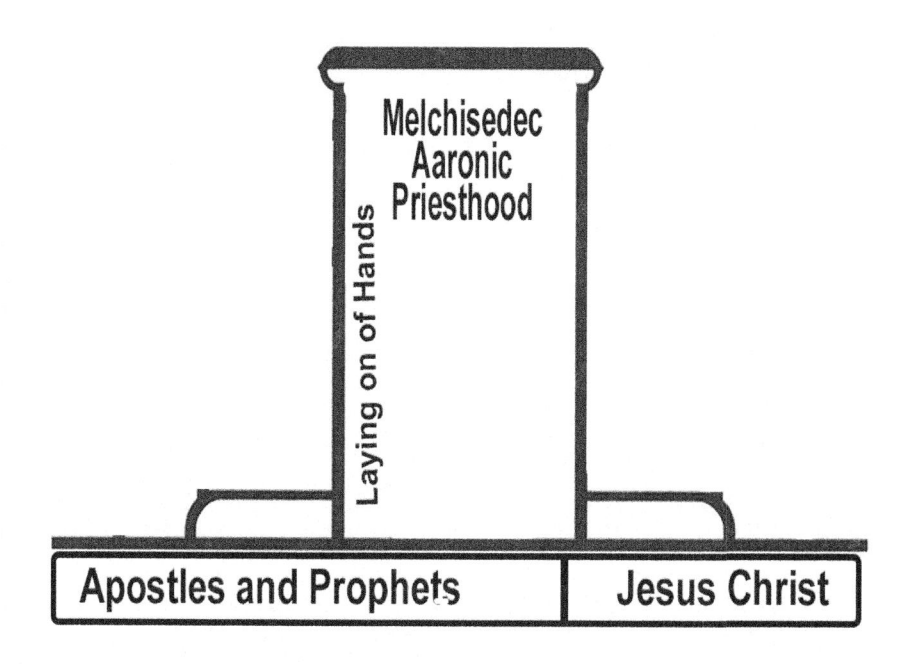

Apostles and Prophets | **Jesus Christ**

Priesthood authority is given only by the laying on of hands by someone who already has that authority. That's how it was done in the original church.

By the way, if we keep reading that scripture it tells us about Simon, who sees the authority and power used to give the gift of the Holy Ghost, and he offers them money so that he can have that authority.

In Acts 8...

18 And when Simon saw that through laying on of the apostles' hands the Holy Ghost was given, he offered them money,

19 Saying, Give me also this power, that on whomsoever I lay hands, he may receive the Holy Ghost.

20 But Peter said unto him, Thy money perish with thee,

because thou hast thought that the gift of God may be purchased with money.

The power or priesthood of God cannot be bought with money - you cannot buy it online - or through a university or church. It is not for sale, the Melchisedec and Aaronic Priesthood are only available if you have been called of God, by one who has that authority, and who gives it to you by the laying on of hands.

The scripture shows above - **The Gift of the Holy Ghost was only given by The Laying on of Hands** (placing hands upon the head of the one receving the Gift of the Holy Ghost). It was not given or received in any other way.

Does anyone even claim to hold the Melchisedec or Aaronic Priesthood today? It was in the original church that Jesus set up. And, even Jesus performed his miracles using this authority.

Having the right authority, to act in the name of God, would seem to be a big deal. Does it exist in any church today?

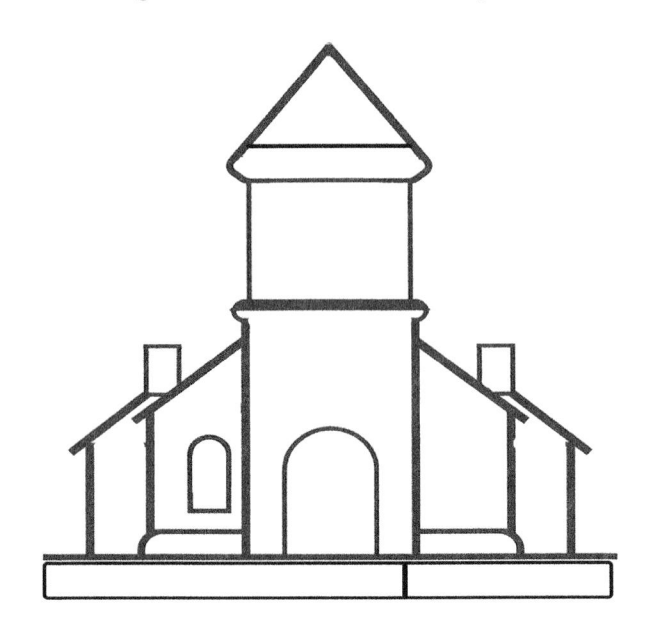

Baptism by Immersion ONLY

Baptism is essential to entering into the Kingdom of God (Heaven). In **John 3:5** it states:

5 Jesus answered, Verily, verily, I say unto thee, Except a man be born of water and of the Spirit, he cannot enter into the kingdom of God.

So, to enter Heaven you must be baptised by water, and by the Spirit (Receive the Holy Ghost).

How was baptism carried out in the original church? Was it by sprinkling, partial immersion, or by full immersion - dipping the whole body under the water?

In **Matthew 3:13-16** it reads:

13 Then cometh Jesus from Galilee to Jordan unto John, to be baptized of him.

14 But John forbad him, saying, I have need to be baptized of thee, and comest thou to me?

15 And Jesus answering said unto him, Suffer it to be so now: for thus it becometh us to fulfil all righteousness. Then he suffered him.

16 And Jesus, when he was baptized, went up straightway out of the water: and, lo, the heavens were opened unto him, and he saw the Spirit of God descending like a dove, and lighting upon him:

Notice that Jesus came straightway our of the water. He had been fully immersed and came all the way out. We are fully immersed under the water to represent the death, buriel and then the resurrection of Jesus. It tells us this in **Romans 6:3-5**

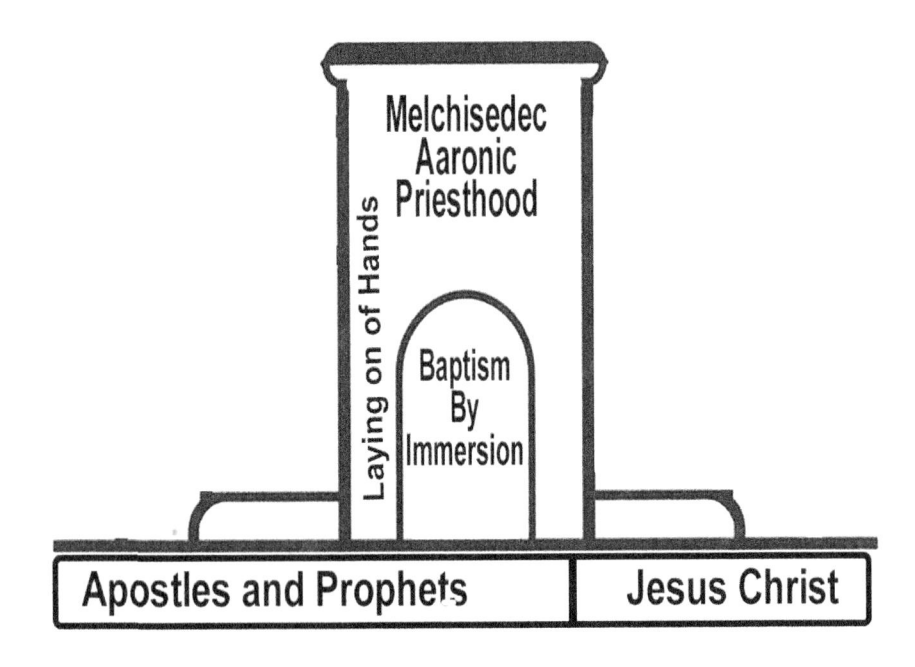

```
          Melchisedec
           Aaronic
          Priesthood

   Laying on of Hands

          Baptism
            By
         Immersion

 Apostles and Prophets    Jesus Christ
```

3 Know ye not, that so many of us as were baptized into Jesus Christ were baptized into his death?

4 Therefore we are buried with him by baptism into death: that like as Christ was raised up from the dead by the glory of the Father, even so we also should walk in newness of life.

5 For if we have been planted together in the likeness of his death, we shall be also in the likeness of his resurrection:

This scripture is very clear that we are buried with Christ under the water, then come out from the water, born again, in the likeness of Jesus's resurrection.

Baptism was carried out by immersion in the early church, and it was only carried out by priesthood authority - in this case by John the Baptist (who held the priesthood authority to perform the baptism).

The Original Church Didn't Pay its Minister or Leaders

Paying church offerings is a practice in most churches today. After all, how is the Minister or Priest supposed to get by without a collection? But, did you know the early leaders of the original church did not get paid. They gave up everything to follow into the ministry, and relied on the kindness of the church membership giving help, but not money.

I bet it would be hard to find anyone today willing to lead a church congregation without getting paid, right?

In **1 Peter 5** it is clear

2 Feed the flock of God which is among you, taking the oversight thereof, not by constraint, but willingly; not for filthy lucre, but of a ready mind;

The apostles went about preaching willingly, and not for money.

In **Matthew 10:8** we read:

8 Heal the sick, cleanse the lepers, raise the dead, cast out devils: freely ye have received, freely give.

The original church had no paid ministry.

Is there a church today where the congregation leaders don't get paid? Where they do it freely, leading their congregations year after year without any pay?

Pillars shown in diagram: Melchisedec Aaronic Priesthood • Laying on of Hands • Baptism By Immersion • No Paid Ministry • Apostles and Prophets • Jesus Christ

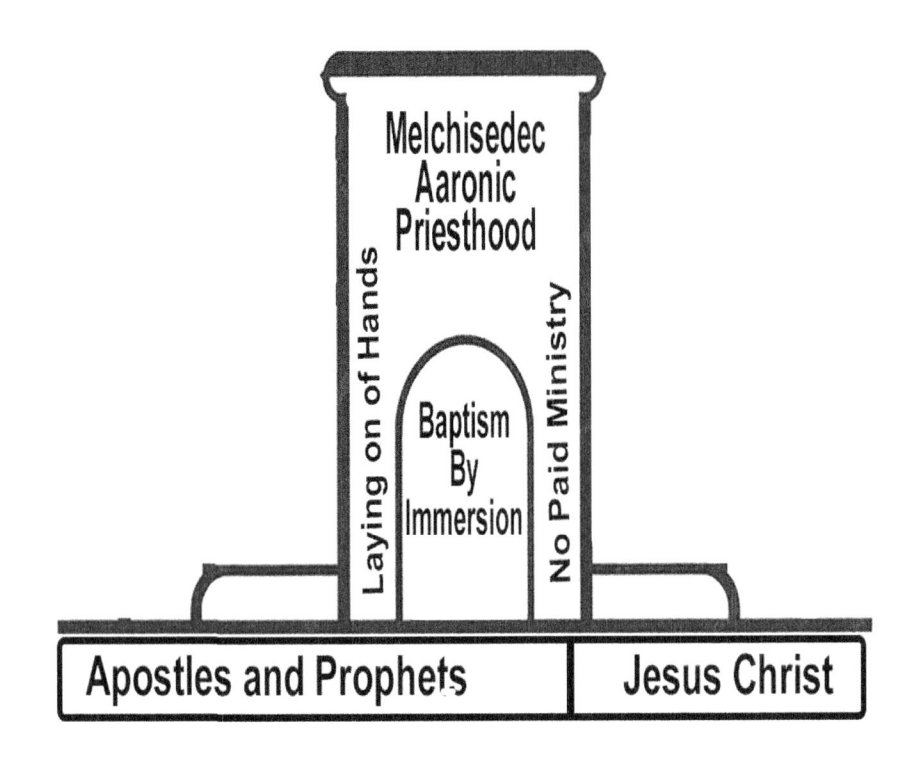

The Church Must Be a Missionary Church

From the very beginning of Christ's church on earth, missionaries were sent across the region, then across the oceans to spread the Gospel message. It was always meant to be like that. **The Church was to be a missionary church.**

In **Matthew 28:19-20** Jesus commanded his disciples to:

19 Go ye therefore, and teach all nations, baptizing them in the name of the Father, and of the Son, and of the Holy Ghost:

20 Teaching them to observe all things whatsoever I have commanded you: and, lo, I am with you alway, even unto the end of the world. Amen.

Missionaries were to travel across into nations to teach the

Gospel, and baptise the believers, in "all nations."

The Original Church was a Missionary Church.

Are there any churches out there still that send tens of thousands of their members out across the world to preach the Gospel - and they do it for absolutely no pay whatsoever? In fact, they save up their own money for years so that they can pay their own way to be full time missionaries - just like Jesus commanded the original church members? That would be quite a commitment in today's 'me, me, me' world.

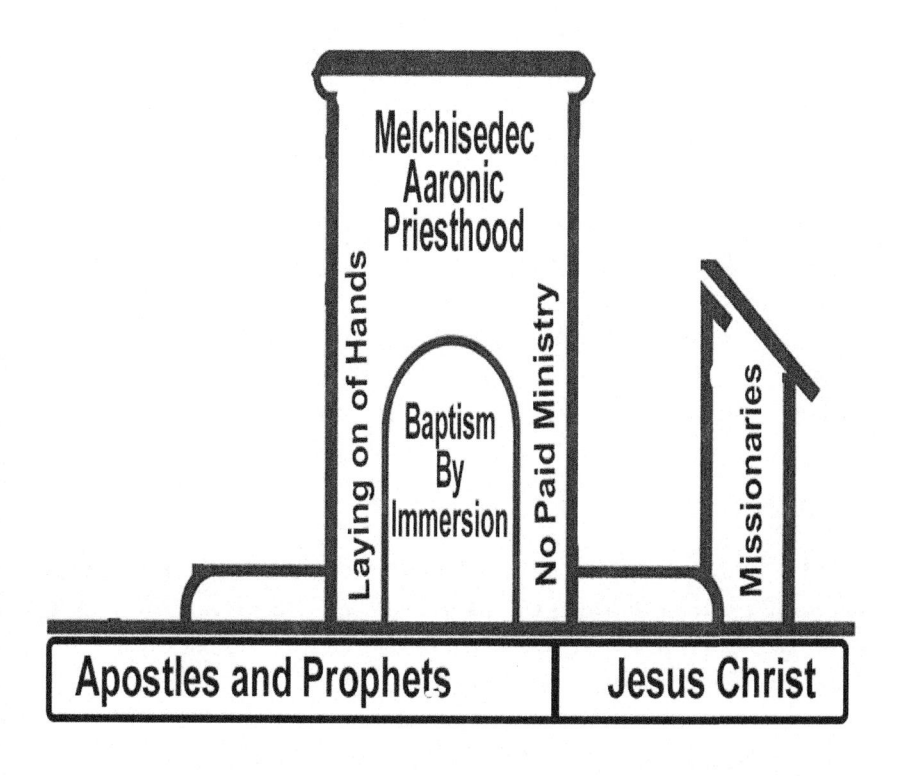

Melchisedec Aaronic Priesthood

Laying on of Hands

Baptism By Immersion

No Paid Ministry

Missionaries

Apostles and Prophets | Jesus Christ

The Original Church Taught about the Gift of The Holy Ghost/Gifts of The Spirit

Having the right priesthood authority to baptiZe or give the gift of the Holy Ghost was essential in the original church. In Acts Chapter 8 it talk about the people in Samaria who heard Phillip preaching the Gospel. They were baptized by him, but not yet received the Gift of the Holy Ghost. Peter and John, who were in Jerusalem heard that people had accepted the Gospel messgae, and been baptised, but had not yet received the Holy Ghost. In **Acts 8:15-17** it says that **Peter and John...**

15 Who, when they were come down, prayed for them, that they might receive the Holy Ghost:

16 (For as yet he was fallen upon none of them: only they were baptized in the name of the Lord Jesus.)

17 Then laid they their hands on them, and they received the Holy Ghost.

Notice that it took the priesthood authority of Peter and John, not Phillip - who came down and *laid their hands on them* - to give them the Gift of the Holy Ghost. Again, notice how it was done in the early church - by the laying on of hands.

Once a member of the church received The Gift of The Holy Ghost by the Laying on of Hands, they were entitled to have one, two or many of those gifts of the Spirit - as recorded in the New Testament.

In **1 Corinthians 12:3-12** Paul describes some of the gifts of the Spirit that can be enjoyed by faithful members of the Church, though not all the gifts are enjoyed by all members. To one member it might be given the Gift of Wisdom, to another the Gift of Healing, to another the Gift of Faith.

3 Wherefore I give you to understand, that no man speaking by the Spirit of God calleth Jesus accursed: and that no man can say that Jesus is the Lord, but by the Holy Ghost.

4 Now there are diversities of gifts, but the same Spirit.

5 And there are differences of administrations, but the same Lord.

6 And there are diversities of operations, but it is the same God which worketh all in all.

7 But the manifestation of the Spirit is given to every man to profit withal.

8 For to one is given by the Spirit the word of wisdom; to another the word of knowledge by the same Spirit;

9 To another faith by the same Spirit; to another the gifts of healing by the same Spirit;

10 To another the working of miracles; to another prophecy; to another discerning of spirits; to another divers kinds of tongues; to another the interpretation of tongues:

11 But all these worketh that one and the selfsame Spirit, dividing to every man severally as he will.

12 For as the body is one, and hath many members, and all the members of that one body, being many, are one body: so also is Christ.

The Original Church taught that the Gift of the Holy Ghost was given by the Laying on of Hands and allowed members to receive special gifts - individual to each member, and not all the same.

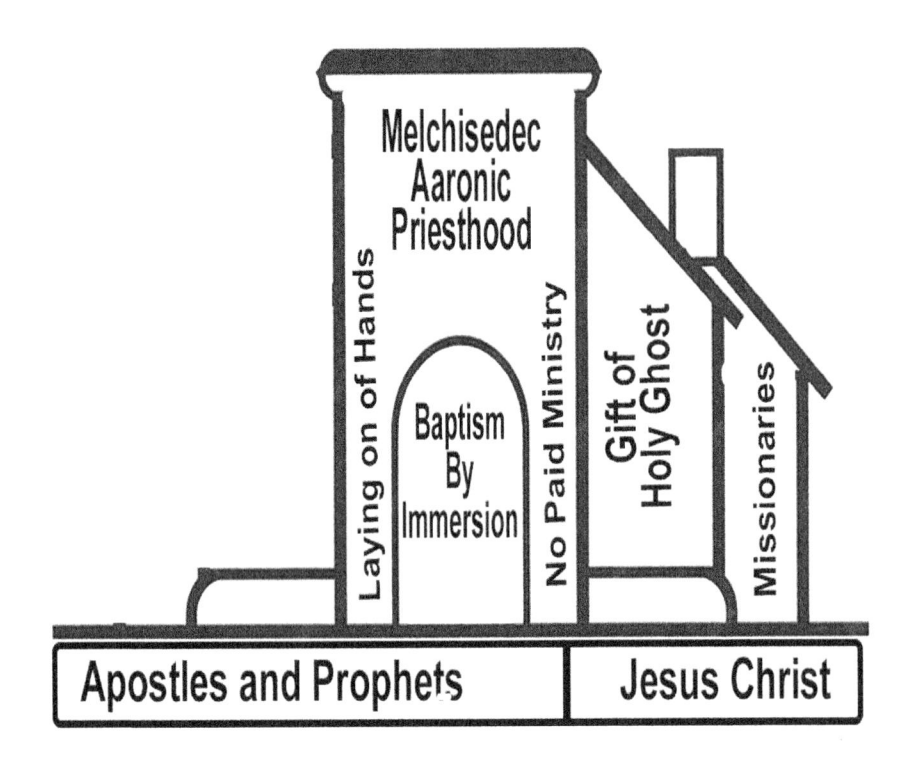

Church structure labels: Melchisedec Aaronic Priesthood | Laying on of Hands | Baptism By Immersion | No Paid Ministry | Gift of Holy Ghost | Missionaries

Foundation: Apostles and Prophets | Jesus Christ

The Original Church Taught that the Gospel would also be Taught in the Spirit World - After Death.

If we accept that you cannot go to Heaven unless you accept Jesus as your Saviour, and be baptized **(John 3:5)** - then what about all those who die without a chance of hearing the Gospel message?

It seems unfair and unjust that a loving Heavenly Father only loves those who have been fortunate enough to live in a country and a time when the Gospel message was preached. What about the millions who lived before Jesus? What about the millions since then that have been born into non Christan nations?

Would a loving Heavenly Father just make Heaven available to just a few lucky ones? No, it makes no sense.

The Original church taught that there is a place where we go - and wait for the Gospel messgae to be taught to us. It's called the Spirit World. We go there after we die - and if we have not heard the Gospel of Jesus in this life - we will be taught the Gospel there - and have a chance to accept or reject it.

This may be a difficult belief for some Christians to accept, probably because they have never heard it before, and because they perhaps haven't read of it in their Bible. But it is there, in black and white.

In **1 Peter 4:6**

6 For for this cause was the gospel preached also to them that are dead, that they might be judged according to men in the flesh, but live according to God in the spirit.

Paul is very clear here, and it cannot be read any other way. This scripture in the Bible says that the Gospel was preached to the dead - so that they can be judged just like us. God has provided a way for ALL of his children to hear the Gospel.

But, is this the only scripture in the New Testament that talks about the place where dead spirits are taught the Gospel? No. In fact, in **1 Peter 3:18-20** it talks about what happened after Jesus was crucified and buried. There was a period of three days before he was resurrected. Do you know what he did during the three days? This scripture reveals just a part of what happened...

18 For Christ also hath once suffered for sins, the just for the unjust, that he might bring us to God, being put to death in the flesh, but quickened by the Spirit:

19 By which also he went and preached unto the spirits

in prison;

20 Which sometime were disobedient, when once the longsuffering of God waited in the days of Noah, while the ark was a preparing, wherein few, that is, eight souls were saved by water.

Jesus, immediately after he was crucified and laid in the tomb, he went and visited the Spirits of the dead in the Spirit World - to teach them the Gospel. He taught the Gospel to those who were now dead, but had lived back in the days of Noah.

The Original Church taught that everyone who has ever lived - will get the chance to hear the Gospel of Jesus Christ - everyone!

Does any church today teach that the dead will hear the Gospel in the Spirit World?

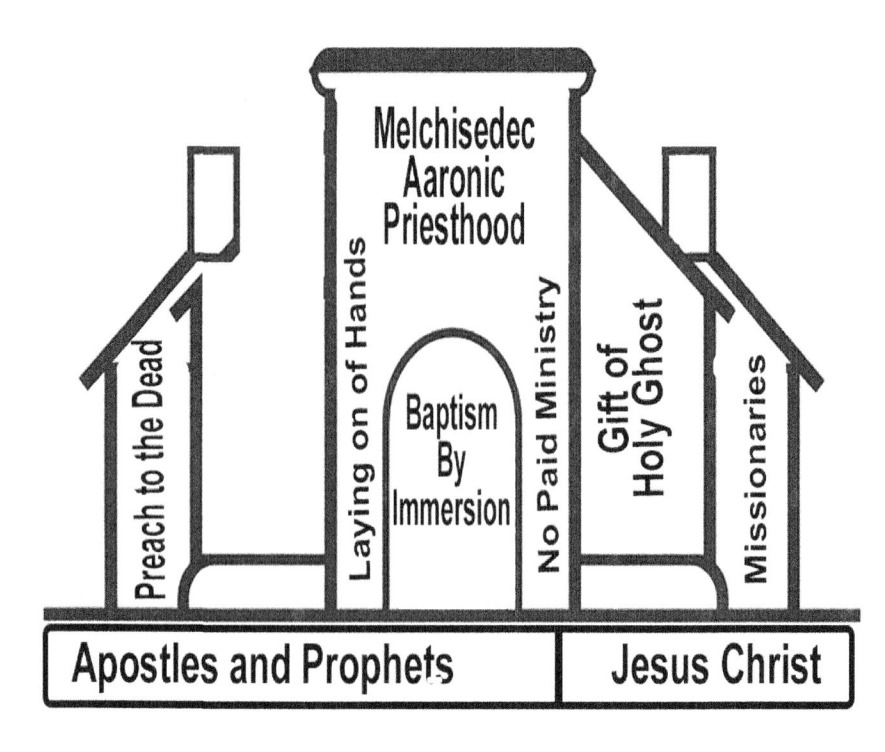

Melchisedec Aaronic Priesthood
Baptism By Immersion
Preach to the Dead
Laying on of Hands
No Paid Ministry
Gift of Holy Ghost
Missionaries
Apostles and Prophets
Jesus Christ

But, What About Baptism? If the Dead Get to Hear the Gospel in the Spirit World - How can They be Baptized to Enter into the Kingdom of Heaven?

We already know in John 3:5 that everyone must be baptized to enter the Kingdom of Heaven, and we now know that the original church taught that everyone will get a chance to hear the Gospel of Jesus Christ, but what if they accept the Gospel, and want to be baptized? It seems unfair for them to know the truth, but still not be able to go to Heaven.

God has provided a way - and it was a belief and practice in the original church that Jesus set up. He knew there would be millions that would not hear His voice directly, and that could not be baptized while on earth - so he taught his Apostles a way they could baptize on behalf of the dead.

Yes, God provided a way, in the original church, and it was taught by his Apostles and practiced by the early members of the church - Baptism for the Dead. Someone would enter the waters of baptism for and on behalf of someone who had already died - so that every person would get the chance to accept or reject the Gospel, and accept or reject the baptism done on their behalf on earth.

In **1 Corinthians 15:16 and 29** we read the question being posed about this sacred practice, noting that the reason it was being carried out in the early church was that the dead also need to rise and be given the chance to enter the Kingdom of Heaven, through Baptism.

This scripture is a discussion about Christ's resurrection, saying that because he rose again, we all can rise again - after death.

16 For if the dead rise not, then is not Christ raised:

17 And if Christ be not raised, your faith is vain; ye are yet in your sins.

20 But now is Christ risen from the dead, and become the firstfruits of them that slept.

21 For since by man came death, by man came also the resurrection of the dead.

22 For as in Adam all die, even so in Christ shall all be made alive.

29 Else what shall they do which are baptized for the dead, if the dead rise not at all? why are they then baptized for the dead?

This powerful scripture gives the reason for carrying out baptisms for those who have died - that everyone will rise again, and they will all be resurrected. If they are to enter the Kingdom of Heaven as Jesus stated in John 3:5, all must hear the Gospel (in the Spirit World) and all must be given the opportunity to be baptized.

Baptism for the dead was taught and carried out in the original Church.

A loving God, who wants all of his children to return to live with him in Heaven, has provided a way for everyone to not only hear the Gospel of Jesus Christ - but an opportunity to accept it and be Baptized.

Does any Church today teach and perform Baptisms for the Dead?

The Original Church of Jesus Christ

Notice how all the pieces are starting to fit together - to create a complete church with
ONE LORD
ONE FAITH
ONE BAPTISM

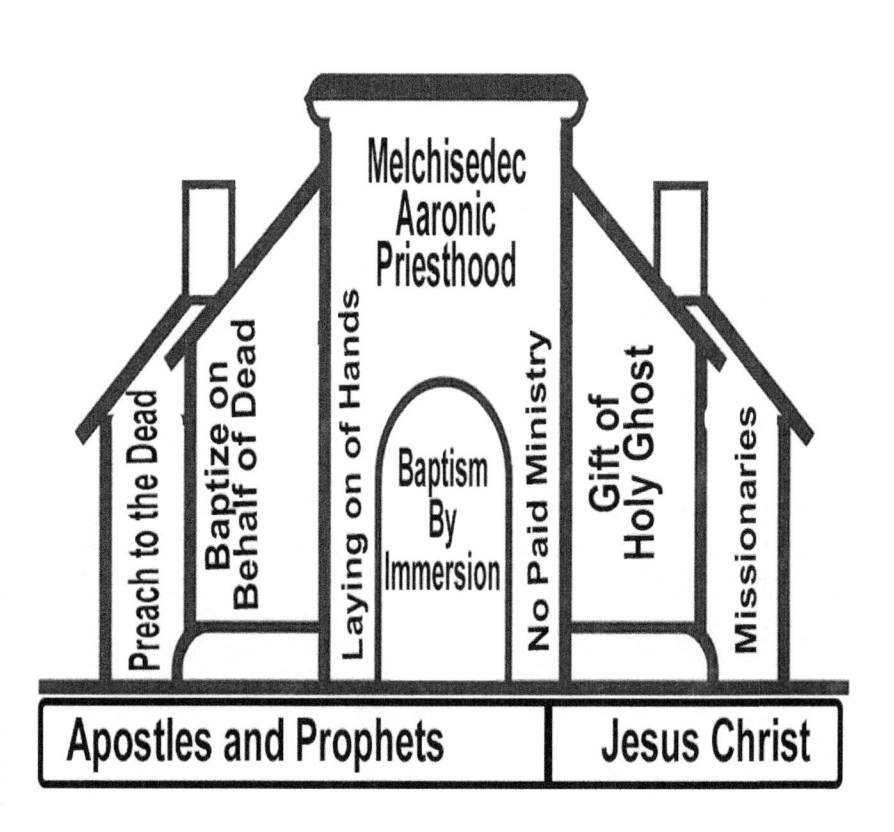

- Preach to the Dead
- Baptize on Behalf of Dead
- Laying on of Hands
- Melchisedec Aaronic Priesthood
- Baptism By Immersion
- No Paid Ministry
- Gift of Holy Ghost
- Missionaries

Apostles and Prophets | **Jesus Christ**

There are 'Three Heavens'

Today, most Christians think of Heaven and Hell as two distinct places, and if you don't make it to Heaven, you are probably going to where it's hot all year round. But, where is the line between Heaven and Hell? Are there certain sins that send you to Hell and other sins that you can commit and still go to Heaven? Where is the rule book so that we can tell where we are going to? It doesn't seem fair or right that there are only two choices of places we are sent, and that we all get thrown together in two big groups, The Good Guys and The Bad Guys.

The Original church taught that within what we would call Heaven, there are at least three distinct places you can be assigned, depending on your faithfulness and commitment to living the Gospel of Jesus Christ.

These three separate areas within Heaven were taught as like comparing the Sun, to the Stars, and to the Moon. The Sun was the highest, brightest or best place to go, where you can dwell with God the Father. The Moon is compared to a lesser glory, where you can dwell with Jesus, and the Stars are compared to an even lower glory - where the Holy Ghost is present.

These different glories - or places within Heven - are all good. They are all part of Heaven. And, even the lower glory is not anywhere near Hell. Hell is a completely different place where the unrighteous, wicked and unrepentant go.

So, where does it talk in the Bible about these three degrees of Glory, or three places within Heaven?

In **1 Corinthians 15:40-42** Paul tells the members of the church that we are resurrected to not one place - but to different degrees of glory.

40 There are also celestial bodies, and bodies terrestrial: but the glory of the celestial is one, and the glory of the terrestrial is another.

41 There is one glory of the sun, and another glory of the moon, and another glory of the stars: for one star differeth from another star in glory.

42 So also is the resurrection of the dead.

We will be judged, and sent to the degree of glory that we have earned. Not all degrees are the same. They differ like the Sun, the Moon and the Stars.

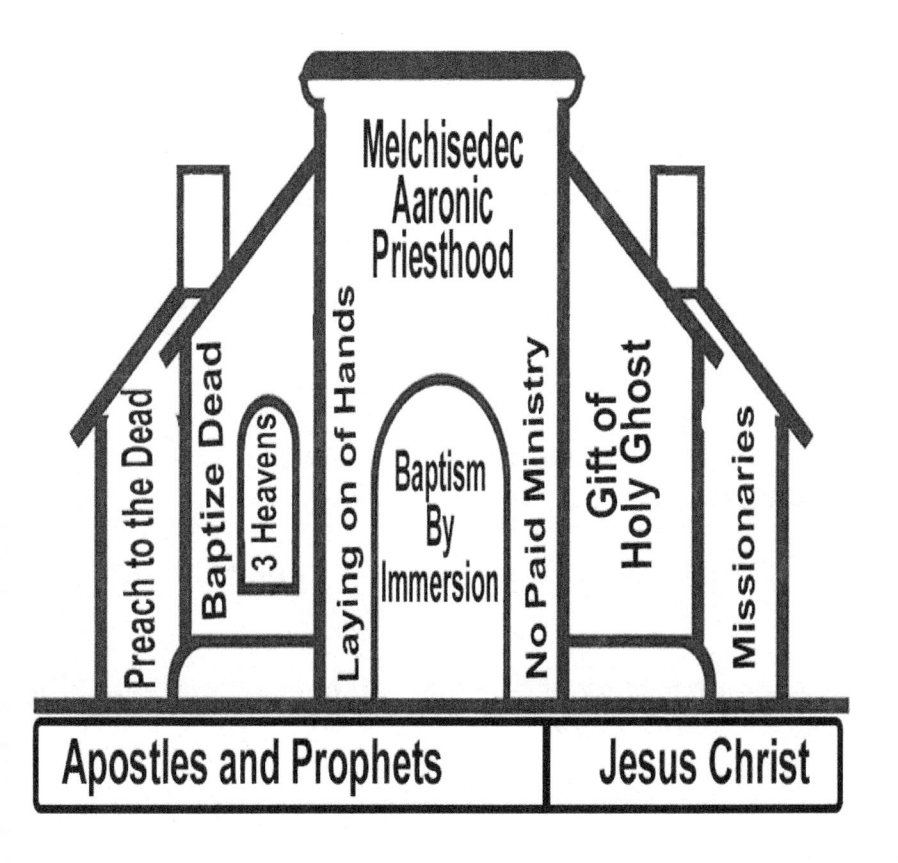

In **2 Corinthians 12:2** the Apostle Paul recalls...

2 I knew a man in Christ above fourteen years ago, (whether in the body, I cannot tell; or whether out of the body, I cannot tell: God knoweth;) such an one caught up to the third heaven.

I bet you've never read that scripture before - referring in the original church to a third Heaven, which means there must be a first and second Heaven. By Paul using the symbols of the sun, the moon, and the stars to describe the different degrees within Heaven, it gave the early members of the church a clearer picture of what Heaven might be like, and also the idea that you don't have to be perfect to make it to Heaven. Even if you are trying your best, there is a place prepared for you. This must have given the original church members much comfort.

The original church taught that Heaven is made up of at least three degrees of glory (or three Heavens) - it is not one place where all the good people go.

This makes a lot of sense, that there isn't just one place and there is a mystery line, above which you go to Heaven, and below which you go directly to Hell. The early church leaders taught what Jesus had taught them,

"In my Father's House there are many mansions."
- **John 14:2**

Did you also notice in verse **42 of 1 Corinthians 15** that it says**,**

"and another glory of the stars: for one star differeth from another star in glory."

This suggests that even within each degree of glory - there are still differences. It suggests that within the place it comnpares to the stars - that even the stars differ in glory to eachother.

So, in the early church the members were taught that you will be judged according to your faithfulness and your good works, and that not all good people receive the same level of glory in Heaven.

In the Original Church the Apostles taught there were at least three Heavens (or degrees of glory within Heaven).

Is there a church out there today that teaches there are three heavens - or degrees of glory?

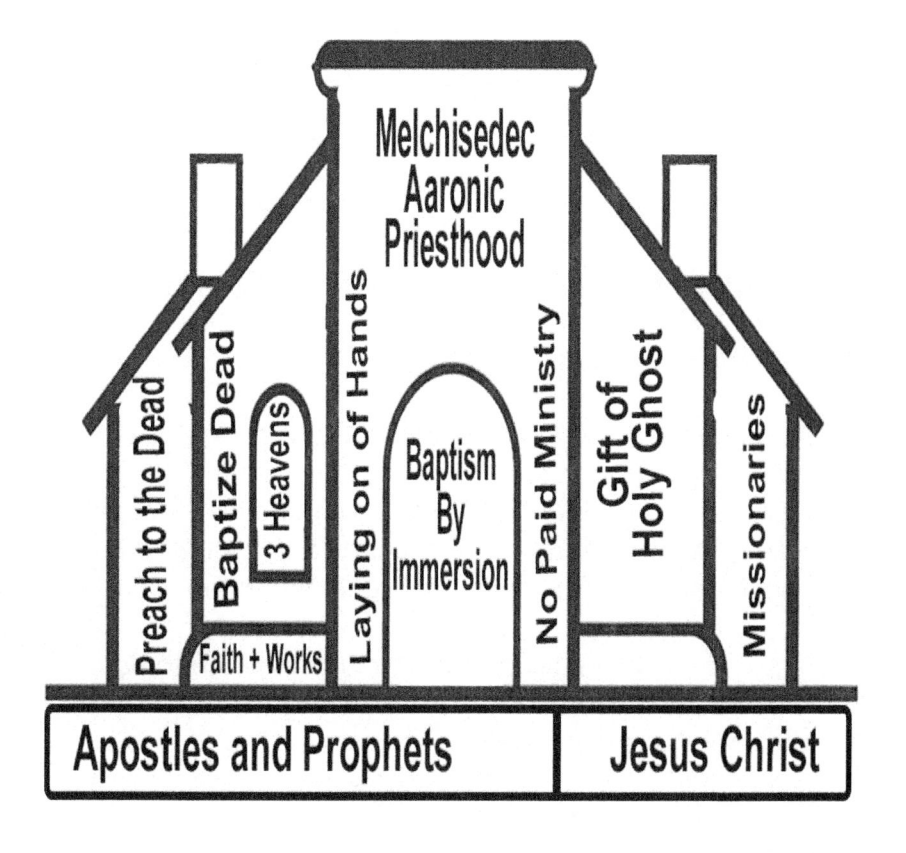

Church diagram showing foundational elements:

- Melchisedec Aaronic Priesthood
- Preach to the Dead
- Baptize Dead
- 3 Heavens
- Faith + Works
- Laying on of Hands
- Baptism By Immersion
- No Paid Ministry
- Gift of Holy Ghost
- Missionaries
- Foundation: Apostles and Prophets | Jesus Christ

Saved by Grace - Or Saved by Works?

What did the original church teach about being saved by the grace of our Lord, Jesus Christ? Some churches today teach that we are all saved by grace, and there is nothing we can do to change that. And so, some teach, our good works don't count for anything because we are saved by Jesus, regarless of what we do.

The original church taught that Jesus died for us and that "his grace is sufficient." True. We are saved from death by the grace of Jesus Christ. His death, buriel and resurrection means that all will be resurrected, will live again, thanks to the grace of Jesus Christ.

But, we are not saved from our sins. We must repent from our sins, and live a good life, trying to do the things Jesus taught.

In **Acts 3:19** it says:

19 Repent ye therefore, and be converted, that your sins may be blotted out, when the times of refreshing shall come from the presence of the Lord;

Jesus paid the penalty for our sins in Gesthemene, so that we wouldn't have to suffer like he did, but he taught, and the Apostles taught that forgiveness for our sins only comes through Repentence - and doing better, living a better life. We must strive to live a better life, repenting often.

In **James 2:17-19** we read that we must continue to do good works, and those that say it is not necessary are vain. It points out that even the devil believes in God. It is not enough to just believe, we must show that belief by the good works that we do in this life.

17 Even so faith, if it hath not works, is dead, being alone.

18 Yea, a man may say, Thou hast faith, and I have works: shew me thy faith without thy works, and I will shew thee my faith by my works.

19 Thou believest that there is one God; thou doest well: the devils also believe, and tremble.

20 But wilt thou know, O vain man, that faith without works is dead?

The original church taught that we are saved from death by grace, but we are only saved from our sins, by repentence, and the good works that we do.

Is there a church today that teaches that faith without works is dead, and that you have to do good works to earn your reward in Heaven?

Will Bad Guys be Resurrected?

Resurrection occurs after death. Our bodies are laid in a grave, and most Christians believe that our Spirit leaves the body.

Resurrection is when the body and spirit come back together. Not all Christians believe in a physical reuniting of the body and the spirit - but it was taught by Jesus and his Apostles.

If you remember, after Jesus was laid in the tomb, just three days later his body was gone. It was missing. But then, Jesus appeared to his family, friends and disciples as a resurrected person, as stated in **Luke 24:39**

39 Behold my hands and my feet, that it is I myself: handle me, and see; for a spirit hath not flesh and bones, as ye see me have.

Jesus was resurrected and was no longer a spirit - his body and spirit had reunited, and his body was now **flesh and bones**. Our resurrected bodies will also be flesh and bones.

Some churches today teach that only the good people, those who have followed Jesus and lived a good life, will have their body and spirit come back together before entering Heaven. But, the original church taught that everyone will be resurrected - good and evil.

In the Corinthians' scripture it talks about how Jesus was the first to be resurrected, and that because he was resurrected, we also will be resurrected. It is His gift to us all.

1 Corinthians 15:21 For since by man came death, by man came also the resurrection of the dead.

In **Acts 24:15** it says that all of us will be resurrected.:

15 And have hope toward God, which they themselves also allow, that there shall be a resurrection of the dead, both of the just and unjust.

The original church taught that ALL will be resurrected - both the good and the bad (the just and the unjust).

But, that does not mean that all will go to Heaven.

Is there a church today that teaches that ALL will be resurrected, both the good and the bad?

Melchisedec Aaronic Priesthood

- Preach to the Dead
- Baptize Dead
- 3 Heavens
- Laying on of Hands
- Baptism By Immersion
- No Paid Ministry
- Gift of Holy Ghost
- Missionaries
- Faith + Works
- ALL Resurrected

Apostles and Prophets | **Jesus Christ**

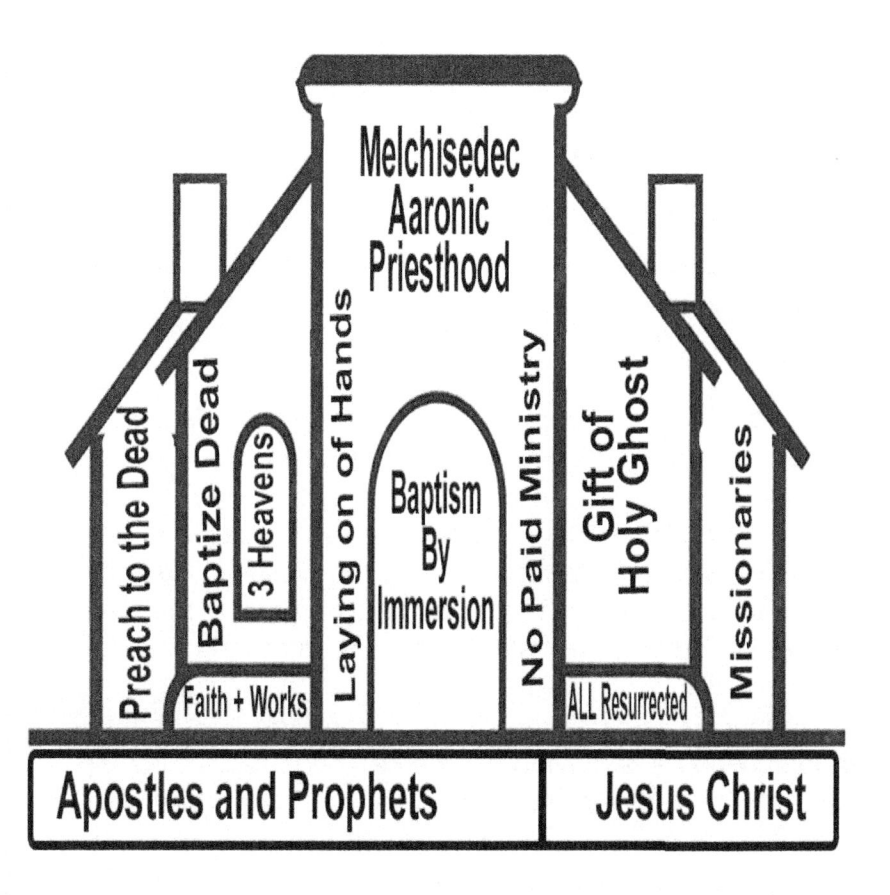

The Original Church Taught that God, Jesus and the Holy Ghost are THREE SEPARATE BEINGS - NOT ONE

This may be difffcult for many Christians to understand, because so many church leaders today teach that God the Father, his son Jesus Christ, and the Holy Ghost are somehow one being, one person.

They are definitely one in purpose - they have the same mission, the same goal. But, the original church, and the Bible teaches that they are three individuals - separate individuals - as separate as you and me.

When Jesus was getting baptized by John the Baptist, do you remember what happened as Jesus entered the water? In **Matthew 3:16-17** we read that the Holy Ghost (Holy Spirit) descended upon Jesus, and then God could be heard from Heaven declaring that "this is my beloved Son".

16 And Jesus, when he was baptized, went up straightway out of the water: and, lo, the heavens were opened unto him, and he saw the Spirit of God descending like a dove, and lighting upon him:

17 And lo a voice from heaven, saying, This is my beloved Son, in whom I am well pleased.

There were three distinct beings...Jesus in the water....the Holy Ghost descends as a dove....and God (the Father) speaks from Heaven. Three individual beings in the same place, but definitely not the same person or being.

In John 17:11 Jesus prays to his Father and asks that the people who he is leaving behind can become one just as He and the Father are one. He clearly doesn't want them to become one person - but one in purpose. He is going to his

Father - but he is not his Father.

11 And now I am no more in the world, but these are in the world, and I come to thee. Holy Father, keep through thine own name those whom thou hast given me, that they may be one, as we are.

In **John 20:17** it states clearly...

17 Jesus saith unto her, Touch me not; for I am not yet ascended to my Father: but go to my brethren, and say unto them, I ascend unto my Father, and your Father; and to my God, and your God.

Jesus is explaining clearly that he is about to ascend to his Father, and he asks Mary Magdalene to tell her brethren that he is about to ascend to his Father - making it clear that they are separate.

The original church taught that God the Father, Jesus the Son, and the Holy Ghost (or spirit) are three individual beings - and not one.

Do churches today teach three individuals, or do they teach that they are three in one? This belief from three individuals to one being was developed/changed early in Christian church history. It is now taught by many Christian religions, but it wasn't what Jesus taught.

The Original Church of Jesus Christ

**Father
Son
Holy Ghost
Seperate**

**Melchisedec
Aaronic
Priesthood**

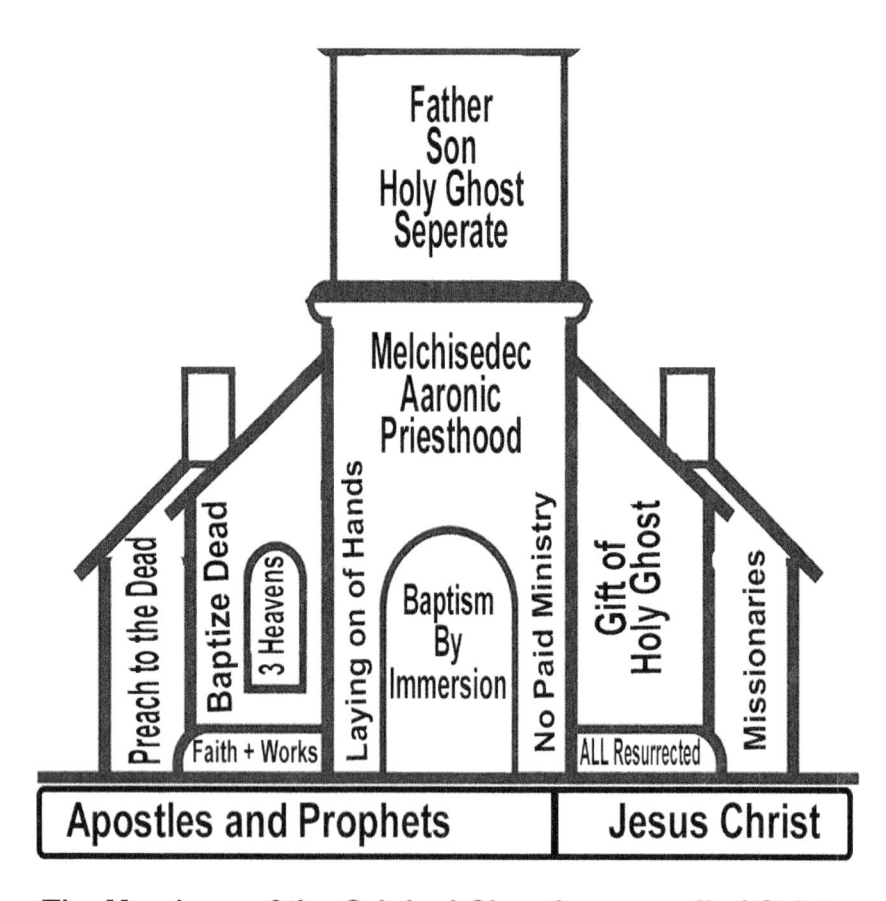

- Preach to the Dead
- Baptize Dead — Faith + Works
- 3 Heavens
- Laying on of Hands
- Baptism By Immersion
- No Paid Ministry
- Gift of Holy Ghost — ALL Resurrected
- Missionaries

Apostles and Prophets | **Jesus Christ**

The Members of the Original Church were called Saints

For many Christians, the word Saint has a very special meaning, and is only reserved for those who are judged to have performed miracles.

But, in the original Church of Jesus Christ - the organisation that He set up, and that his Apostles taught in the first 50 or so years after Jesus died, **ALL MEMBERS OF THE**

ORIGINAL CHURCH WERE CALLED SAINTS.

In Ephesians 2:19 it states, of people when they are baptized and join the Church, that they become...

19 Now therefore ye are no more strangers and foreigners, but fellowcitizens with the saints, and of the household of God;

In the Original Church, ALL members of the church were called Saints once they were Baptized.

Does any church today call ALL of its members Saints, just like the original Church?

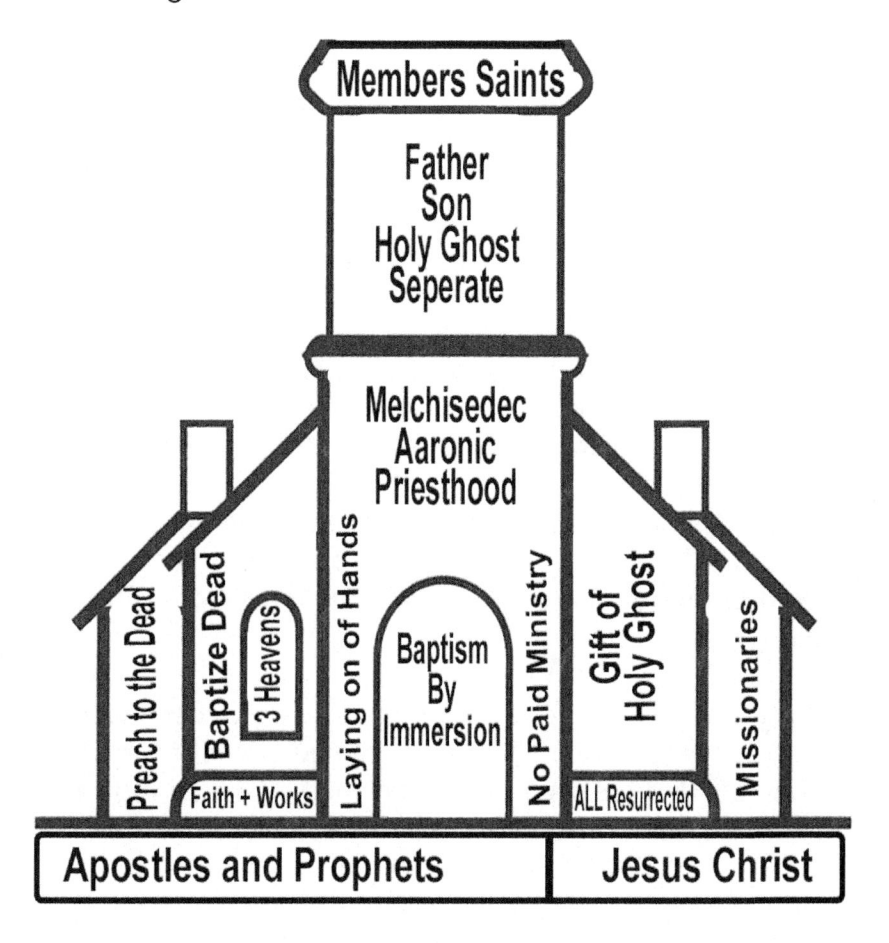

Members Saints

Father
Son
Holy Ghost
Seperate

Melchisedec
Aaronic
Priesthood

Preach to the Dead | Baptize Dead | 3 Heavens | Laying on of Hands | Baptism By Immersion | No Paid Ministry | Gift of Holy Ghost | Missionaries

Faith + Works | ALL Resurrected

Apostles and Prophets | Jesus Christ

The Original Church would Fall Away
- But then Be Restored

Members of the original church were taught that the church that Jesus had set up would not last, that members would fall away, that the truth would be lost, and that the priesthood authority would be lost off the land. Early church leaders taught that the church would be missing from the earth, and would have to be restored in its fullness.

In Paul's letter to the Thessalonians we read in **2 Thessalonians 2** - talking about when Jesus would come again....

1 Now we beseech you, brethren, by the coming of our Lord Jesus Christ, and by our gathering together unto him,

2 That ye be not soon shaken in mind, or be troubled, neither by spirit, nor by word, nor by letter as from us, as that the day of Christ is at hand.

3 Let no man deceive you by any means: for that day shall not come, except there come a falling away first, and that man of sin be revealed, the son of perdition;

4 Who opposeth and exalteth himself above all that is called God, or that is worshipped; so that he as God sitteth in the temple of God, shewing himself that he is God.

Clearly, the early leaders taught that Christ's Second Coming would not happen until after there had been a falling away of the truth and beliefs and authority of the Church. So much so, that the devil himself would be revealed within the teachings and doctrine of some of the churches.

The Original Church of Jesus Christ

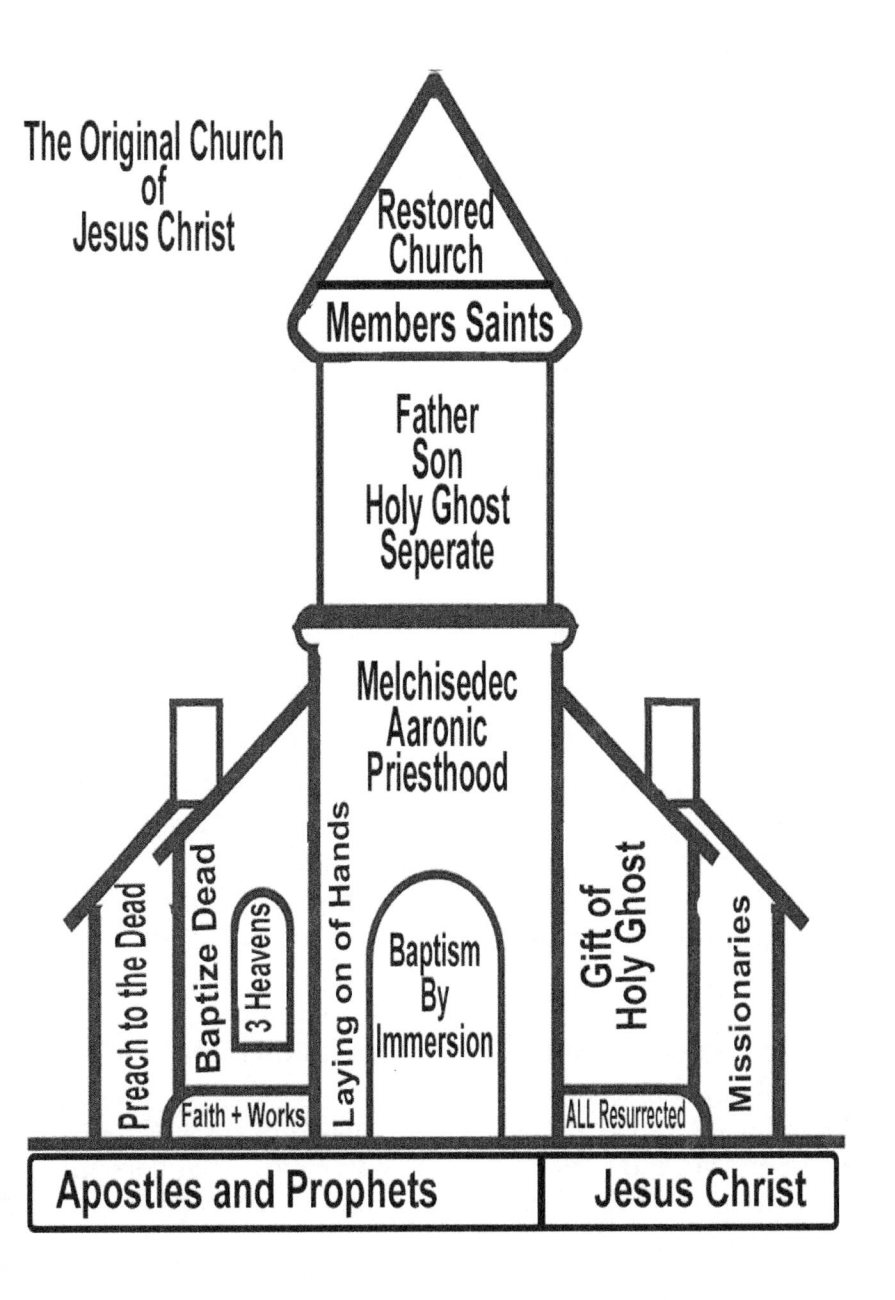

- Restored Church
- Members Saints
- Father Son Holy Ghost Seperate
- Melchisedec Aaronic Priesthood
- Preach to the Dead
- Baptize Dead
- 3 Heavens
- Laying on of Hands
- Baptism By Immersion
- Gift of Holy Ghost
- Missionaries
- Faith + Works
- ALL Resurrected
- Apostles and Prophets
- Jesus Christ

Does this Original Church of Jesus Christ Exist Today?

The original Church of Jesus Christ had many parts. The most important was the foundation of Prophets and Apostles. If you remove the foundation of a building, it will collapse and break apart. That's what happened to the original Church of Jesus Christ.

Once the Apostles and Prophets were no longer on earth, to use their priesthood authority to direct and administer the Gospel principles and sacred ordinanaces, the crumbling church broke into pieces.

Good people came along and wanted to do the right thing, continue the teachings of Jesus, but they didn't have that priesthood authority, and most importantly, without a Prophet on earth, as there always had been, there was no Heavenly direction - God speaking to a living Prophet.

You cannot build a church on one or two bricks of the original. Once the foundation was gone, good men would grab hold to a piece of the original church - for example - baptism by full immersion. They would argue, "it is not being taught in the church that I belong to, and I know it is what Jesus taught - So I cannot carry on going to my church - I will start another one that does believe in baptism by full immersion."

But you cannot build a church with only one piece of truth, or two pieces of the original Gospel. And, without the foundation of a living prophet - you can see why the churches started to disagree with eachother - and split apart - and more and more men started a new branch of Christianity. 45,000 of them at least.

Again, what about Gifts of the Holy Ghost - as taught in the New Testament? Many churches don't teach about the gifts, and believe they were only a thing of the past. So, new churches sprung up that featured heavily on the gifts of the

Spirit. But, that was only one piece of the original church.

There are churches today that send out missionaries - hundreds of them. Some missionaries are paid, some are part time, operating in their local town or city a few hours a month. This is good, but it is still only another piece of the original church.

Of the 45,000 or more different Christian denominations in the world, do any of them have all of the pieces of the original church? Do they have a few pieces, but are still missing the foundation, the walls, the windows, a roof, a door?

There had to be a complete restoration of the Original Church of Jesus Christ. It had to be restored with every single brick of that original church. Starting with the foundation - the calling of a living Prophet, and 12 living Apostles. Jesus had to be the very cornerstone and head of the restored Church. It had to have that original priesthood authoriy - including a restoration of the Melchisedec and Aaronic Priesthood. If it didn't. it would not have the correct authority to carry out any of the ordinances and principles of the original church.

If the Church of Jesus Christ was to be restored, it would have to teach that the dead can be taught the Gospel, and it would have to provide an opportunity for baptisms for the dead to be carried out.

That church would have to teach that there are at least three Heavens, that everyone will be resurrected - even the unjust, the members would be called Saints, and its local church leaders would head up the church for free, for no financial reward, and it would teach that God the Father, his son Jesus Christ, and the Holy Ghost are three, distinct, individual beings.

Could there be such a church on earth today? A fully restored original church of Jesus Christ?

Surely, any Christian, searching for the truth, and wanting to follow the original church that Jesus Christ set up, would want to search and search until they found such a church - if it did exist..

The good news is that the restored Church of Jesus Christ is in full operation today, all over the world, and there is probably one near to where you live.

The Church of Jesus Christ of Latter Day Saints is the restored original Church of Jesus Christ, and it is led by a living Prophet and 12 Apostles who receive direct revelation from God to lead. The world again has a living Prophet.

The Latter Day Saint Church has all the pieces of the original church, fully restored. All those teachings that we have found in the New Testament, that were taught by the original Apostles and local leaders of the original church, have been restored, and are now being taught by leaders of the Church of Jesus Christ of Latter Day Saints.

They even have special temples dotted all across the earth, where baptisms for the dead are carried out, and they have invested millions of dollars in setting up family research centres, so that you can research your ancestry, and provide an opportunity for them to hear and accept the Gospel, and accept baptism performed on their behalf.

The Melchisedec and Aaronic priesthood have been restored, and boys from the age of 12 can receive the lesser (Aaronic) priesthood so that they can carry out some of the administrative jobs within the church. Older males hold the Melchisedec Priesthood which gives them authority to perform many sacred ordinances - just like in the original church. It is the same Priesthood that Jesus held.

It is a church that believes in modern day miracles, just like the church of old, and blessings are given, using the priesthood power, to heal the sick. Priesthood power is passed down from those who hold that authority, and it is done by the laying on of hands, in accordance with the original church.

And, to show that faith also requires good works, the modern day Church of Jesus Christ has a massive charitable arm that donates over $1.3 billion per year in money, goods and services to aid Humanitarian Relief Projects across the world - including efforts to eradicate diseases and provide clean drinking water. They do it just like Jesus did - quietly, behind the scenes, without blowing their own trumpet.

Volunteers are sent out from the church to help in areas of need and disaster - and church members are often the first ones on scene at major disasters such as floods, earthquakes and hurricanes. The church has strategically placed aid centres and trucks that distribute aid in emergencies. It is a Church that firmly believes in faith plus good works.

The modern day church sends out over 72,000 full time missionaries - who leave their jobs, studies, homes and loved ones to serve wherever they are called worldwide. These young and older missionaries leave the comforts of their home for up to 2 years of full time service, preaching the Gospel, or serving on humantarian missions. And, just like in the original church - they go "without purse or script" and they pay for themselves to be there..

The original Church of Jesus Christ has been restored in its fullness. It contains all those things that Jesus and His Apostles taught in the early church, as we have found in the

New Testament of the Bible. Even doctrine that was difficult to find, and things that we have never seen before - and yet it is all there, in our Bible - and in The Church of Jesus Christ of Latter Day Saints.

Although we have covered a lot of parts to the original church - there are so many more parts of the original church that have been restored. For example, the building of Temples was a big part of the Old and New Testament. Temples are where sacred services, such as Baptism for the Dead, are performed. The modern day Church of Jesus Christ has more than 190 temples operating across the world, and has plans for another 43 under construction - as of 2024.

The modern day church teaches Faith, Repentence, Baptism and the Gift of the Holy Ghost by the Laying on of Hands, and then encourages its members to serve others. Each Sunday, members gather in local church building to take the sacrament - the bread and water - in remebrance of the Saviour - just as he broke bread and gave it to His disciples in the days before His crucifixtion.

They teach that we are all the sons and daughters of a loving, Heavenly Father - and that we lived with him as spirits before we came to this earth - and that life is a learning place - where we prepare to return to live with Him again. These were all taught in the original church.

Members pay Tithing (just as taught in the Bible) and they live by a Health Code - and they believe that marriage is not "until death do you part" - but that marriages and families can be together forever - another purpose of Holy Temples.

No other church in the world has **all** the parts of the original church fully restored - every single belief that Jesus and His Apostles taught. Yes, the original church has been restored.

The Original Church of Jesus Christ

Restored Church

Members Saints

Father
Son
Holy Ghost
Seperate

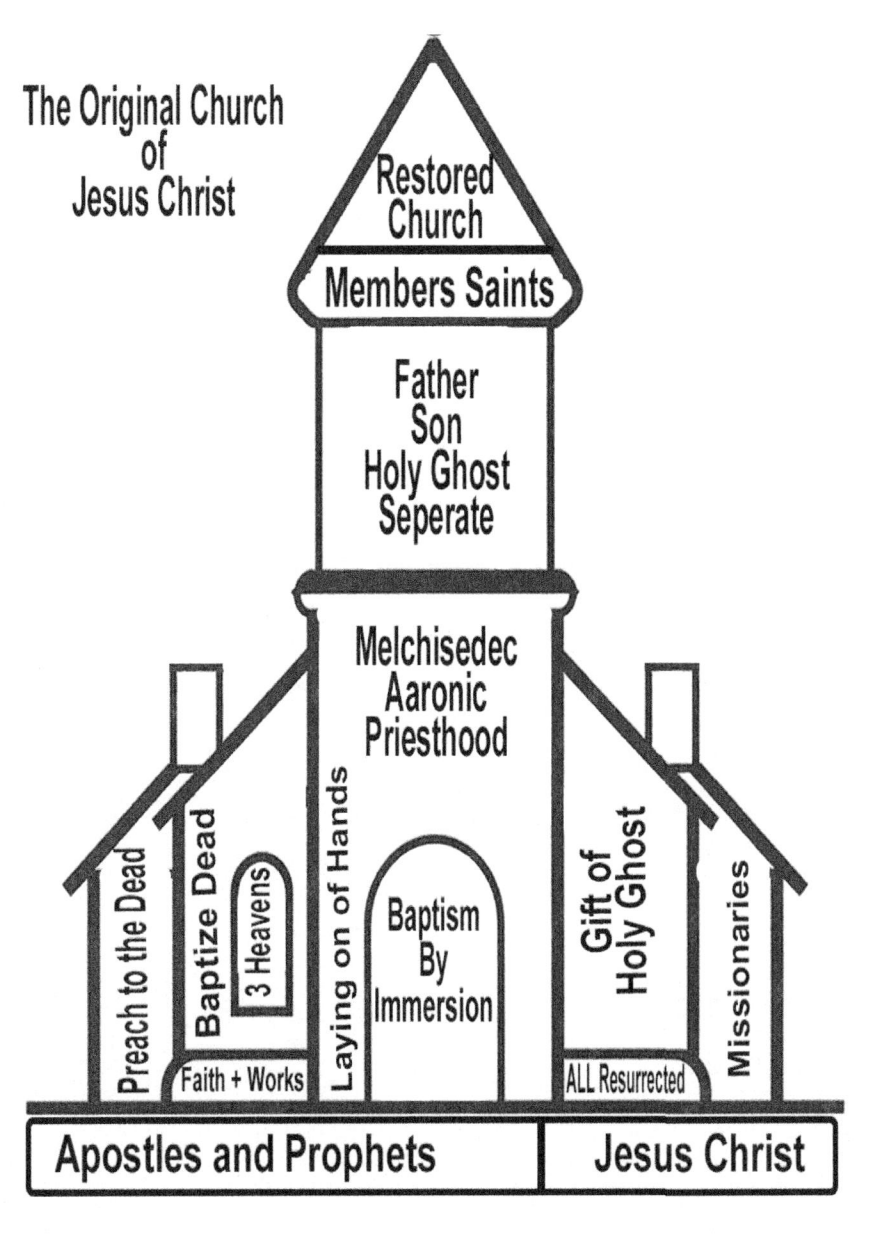

Melchisedec
Aaronic
Priesthood

- Preach to the Dead
- Baptize Dead
- 3 Heavens
- Laying on of Hands
- Baptism By Immersion
- Faith + Works
- Gift of Holy Ghost
- ALL Resurrected
- Missionaries

Apostles and Prophets | **Jesus Christ**

This is the Church of Jesus Christ of Latter Day Saints
- The Lord's Restored Original Church

Printed in Great Britain
by Amazon